READER BONUS

Your investment in this book entitles you to a very special gift that is the foundation of Author Podcasting™

It is a seven-part recording of an exclusive training, "Building Your Media Kit," where attendees invested $197 to participate, and you can have it as my gift to you!

The training goes into greater detail on how to make your media kit in Google documents with over-the-shoulder tutorials and explains the importance of having active links and hashtags for your business and social media marketing.

DOWNLOAD TODAY!

AuthorPodcasting.com/readerbonus

Author Podcasting

Be a Stand-Out Guest While Taking Your Book on a Virtual Tour

Janine Bolon

ALSO BY JANINE BOLON

Seeking the Divine, Vol. 1

Finding the Divine, Vol. 2

Expressing the Divine, Vol. 3

Creating with the Divine Vol. 4 (2022)

The Thriving Solopreneur

Money...It's Not Just for Rich People!

Ditching Debt

The Grocery Store Game

Cash, Cars & College: a YA Guide to Financial Freedom

10 Steps to Abundance: Mindful Money Mastery

To Bryan Hyde & Shawn Denevan,
the men who taught me how podcasting really works!

Published under the Copyright Laws of the Library of Congress of The United States of America, by:

The8Gates, LLC
1727 Main Street, #6386
Longmont, CO 80501-7311
720-684-6535

072221

CONTENTS

Foreword 1

Who Should Read This Book? 3

My Promise 9

Introduction 11

What is a Media Kit? 15

Building a Media Kit 19

Start with a Google Document 21
Your Header 22
Table of Contents 23
Headshots 25
Book Images 26
Quotes 27
Bios 28
Topics of Conversation 29
Testimonials 30
Interview Questions 30
Course Description 32
Social Media Links 32
Hashtags 34

After the Interview **35**

Your Social Media 36

Promoting the Show 37

Follow Up with the Show Host 37

Taking Your Book on Tour **39**

Time to Make a List 40

Pick Your Top Three Topics 41

Gather Podcasts 42

Finding Podcasts Through Readers & Colleagues 45

Finding Podcasts Through iTunes & Spotify 47

Case Study #1: Chris Riedel **51**

Case Study #2: Jade Alexander **59**

Case Study #3: Meredith Bell **67**

The Media Checklist **81**

The Next Step—Be My Guest **83**

About Janine Bolon **87**

Podcast Resources **89**

Connect With Me **91**

FOREWORD

Janine Bolon is a powerhouse of audio, authorship and promotion. In *Author Podcasting*, she uses her knowledge of all three to provide readers an excellent, but elegantly simple, step-by-step guide to becoming a dream guest for podcasters.

Having had my own podcast at one time, one of my biggest frustrations was a guest who could not seamlessly provide me with the details required to produce the show simply and easily. A bio needs to be a brief read, not a page-long Word document. A headshot needs to be of high-quality, not a selfie or photo that crops out others.

Janine uses her years of experience in all angles of production and synthesizes what authors need to know before embarking on their virtual podcast book tours. She walks them through the process of developing a proper media kit and explains why each element is necessary.

Once authors have followed her process for the kit, she provides great recommendations on how to expand the universe of podcasters they'll want to reach out to. This is key to success.

If you want to sell books, it is not enough to be interviewed a few times. You will want to develop a robust interview schedule and relationships with those who interview you. Doing so leads to more contacts, connections, leads and ultimately sales.

As an author, I feel lucky to have connected with Janine and her wisdom at just the right time. This book takes disparate pieces of marketing knowledge from the recesses of my brain and brings all of it to the forefront tying it up in a beautiful bow.

With a strong media kit, a great strategy, and a good message, you can become a podcaster's favorite guest. Your message is already in your book. The keys to the rest are in *Author Podcasting*.

Suzanne Tregenza Moore
Strategic Entrepreneurial Marketing Coach
June 2021

WHO SHOULD READ THIS BOOK?

Even though this book is designed to be read in about an hour, I don't want to waste your time if it's not a good fit. Please take a few minutes and read this entire section to see if *Author Podcasting* is a smart investment of your time and focus. I wrote this quick read for three reasons:

1. To shift your focus from writing your book to promoting your book.
2. To share with you the tips and techniques I learned over the last 17 years on how to market your book through podcasting.
3. To invite you to connect with me to determine if working together is our next step.

People in today's climate are seeking high-quality information to make smart decisions, save time and avoid mistakes. Or they are seeking engaging content to help them escape the challenges of their daily lives. You and your book can do this for them. I want to help you expand your reach for your particular genre while sustaining an organic growth in your readership that will keep you in the business of writing for as long as you enjoy working on your next book.

I am unapologetically "selling" in this book, not only the concept of promoting your book through podcasting guest appearances but also why working directly with me to get your professional habits streamlined is a smart and effective shortcut to success and quick completion of your writing and marketing accountability.

If you're good with all this so far, allow me to further drill down into what type of writer I've written this book for and who I know can benefit from the information inside.

I believe just about any writer will profit from having this system of media kit build-outs for their book promotions, but there are four "types" who are ideal.

1. You're working full-time and you only have a few hours a week you can spend "marketing" your books; after all, you really want to spend as much time as possible writing the next book!

2. You're starting to wrap-up your debut novel and you have no idea how to market your book.
3. You've had a major life event occur (loss of job, parent/partner needs home care, etc.), and you've decided now is the time to dust off those book ideas that you've had sitting around for decades. Before writing your book, you're looking into how to incorporate marketing into the book itself.
4. You're working full time, and you've invested in a MLM (Arbonne®, Mary Kay®, doTerra®, Young Living®, Youngevity®, etc.), and you really wish to grow your side business (MLM: multi-level marketing program) by writing a quick book to train those team members on the ropes. Now that you've done that, it is time to promote you and your book.

These four types of writers have unique needs to explain, clarify and position their products and/or services, which I believe are best served with a simple, easy-to-do system of marketing their book through the podcasting systems.

Finally, *Author Podcasting* was written for the person who agrees with these seven beliefs:

1. Time is the most precious gift in our lives, and if we can connect and help others while taking up less time, we will be rewarded.
2. The written word containing useful information is one of the best ways to communicate why your book(s) will help others solve a problem, take advantage of a new opportunity, or give a bit of entertainment to escape real life for a mini vacation in your story.
3. Sharing your personal story and stories of how you have helped others will uniquely humanize you and be the beginning of a mutually beneficial relationship between you and your readers.
4. You only have a moment to grab the interest of your targeted prospective readers/ listeners amid the onslaught of competing marketing messages they are exposed to every day. Once you have their attention with your message or book example in their hands, you will have a more focused opportunity to communicate why they should invest in your books or newsletter.
5. A real, professionally "constructed" media kit is one of the most powerful advantages and unique game changers in the podcast-

ing world for positioning you and attracting more ideal readers.

6. A custom system for podcasting promotion of your book(s) is an asset for you to create, and working with me is the key to getting it done fast and implemented pain-free in your own book marketing cycle.
7. Being a podcast guest is a great way to take your book on a virtual tour, and you want to learn how.

If you are like me and believe you can make a difference in people's lives with your writing, and you are not afraid of making specific "next-step offers" for your readers to take, I wrote this book for you, so please keep reading.

MY PROMISE

I promise to make *Author Podcasting* a valuable use of your money, time and attention. Within the next 60 minutes or so, my intention is to open your eyes to the opportunities that await you as you build your media kit for the podcasting tour you can do for your book launch. This activity will make you a fantastic guest for most podcasters.

I will minimize the hype and bloat (found in a lot of business books), get right to the point and share the essentials of what you need to know as an author who is in charge of your own marketing. And trust me, no one is going to promote your book as much as you can. Before we move on, I have two reminders for you. Regardless of whether you call the people you write for, "readers," "listeners," or "customers," I'll be calling them "readers" through the rest of this book.

Also, I am not going to spend much time trying to convince you that you need to spend time building your media kit. A simple scan of books around podcasting, marketing and the changes in publishing will reveal many options to you on the importance of virtual book launches through the use of podcasting and online events.

Now to the magic of promotion through the use of your media kit.

INTRODUCTION

Congratulations! You've finished writing your book! You deserve a huge pat on the back and a hearty exclamation of, "Well done!"

I became a published author in 2005. I self-published my first book, *Money...It's Not just for Rich People!* This book came about after years of teaching families and students the principles necessary to become financially independent and debt-free. At the time, there was little written about self-publishing, and I knew nothing about how to market myself, my book or my 60/40 principle for wealth accumulation. I saved my money and bought a $2,500 marketing package from a trusted marketing agency, and I was launched into the world of marketing and promotion through public appearances on television, radio, and speaking events. It was a whirlwind of emails, phone calls and travel, but the book got into the hands of the right people, and I was able to sell 7,000 copies. This is a huge number considering I was working part-time as a college professor and homeschooling my 4 children who were all under the age of 11.

Over the course of time, I was highlighted on MSNBC and other shows and had offers to appear on The Oprah Winfrey Show. However, after our first phone interview, the show's producers told me, "Sorry, Janine, you're not sexy enough for the show we're doing." Please understand, they were saying it as a joke. And later, when I saw the show they ran, they were right. I was not at all a good fit for their episode. They were interested in extreme frugality, and that was not a principle I taught. So, back I went to appearances on radio shows and book signings at local shops within a 3-hour drive of my home. I found that it was easier to get on radio shows, and I started to have a following as people heard my interviews. I was surprised at how many folks actually listened to talk radio since I had never been a fan of that medium.

In 2007, I got involved in "audioblogging" or BlogTalkRadio as the platform was called and started a show called *Women of Power* and launched programs that aired monthly. I had sponsors and free materials that were given out as corporations marketed to this new niche of audio bloggers. It was in 2017, when I changed platforms and became a professional "podcaster" with *The Practical Mystic Show* and my radio career came full circle with weekly episodes. By 2020, I was broadcasting to 27 different platforms and had added 3 additional shows, *3 Minute Money Tips*, *The Thriving Solopreneur*, and *The Writers Hour Creative Conversations*.

I share this with you to let you know that podcasting is by far the most fun I've had as an author. I've enjoyed being interviewed by others as well as interviewing guests. However, one of the things that I have noticed as I've reached out to folks to be on my shows was the lack of media kits. This was something I learned early on when working with television producers and event planners. In order to introduce you, your message and your book properly, these media professionals and show hosts require a media kit. If you don't have any idea what I'm talking about, let's fill you in now.

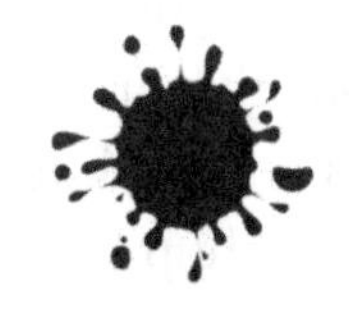

WHAT IS A MEDIA KIT?

Media kits are the more modern version of traditional "press kits" that used to be handed out to reporters and newspaper offices in a cardboard folder. The folder would be filled with pages of documentation containing information about your business, product or event that you wanted to have highlighted by the "press."

Press kits were mainly used at events and for launches as a package of information that would help journalists write their story because all the pertinent information and contact details were laid out for them along with a pre-written "press release" to give them all the resources they needed to make their publishing deadlines. The point of the old press kit was to catch the eye of journalists and make them want to write up a positive article or to follow up with the organizer to do a feature interview. The press kits of old were a one-stop shop for all of the information a journalist would need to accomplish their work.

We are now operating in the age of the digital world with websites, social media and internet-based media and broadcasts. Events are held online through webinars, Zoom, Facebook Live and LinkedIn "events." The press kit has been replaced by the "media kit" in order to keep up with the technology and needs of the times. A media kit serves one function: to assist in your promotion of you, your message and your book. It is a single document that has all the information an interviewer or event planner will need to make a decision as to whether or not you should be placed on their agenda, episode or news program. The contents of any media kit should have the basic outline or "skeleton" of a framework that all serve the needs of the host, event planner or interviewer in promoting you and your book.

Media kits do not take long to put together. You probably have all the information you need right now. But the challenge is getting them in a format your people can use as they host you on their platforms. As we move through the different sections of the media kit, know that we are focusing on digital media platforms where they need all your information accessible and customizable to their image constraints and space limitations.

As we move forward through this process of creating your media kit and working with the professionals who require such things, remember this one important fact: When you state to an event planner, radio show host or interviewer, "Would you like my media kit?", that immediately causes their shoulders to drop from the stress they carry around because they now know they are dealing with a professional who understands their deadlines. You are a cut above! You understand the promotional process.

BUILDING YOUR MEDIA KIT

The type of media kit that I'm going to be discussing with you is completely digital. This media kit will be usable in almost all areas of your promotion for your book and business.

Consider it like a resume for your project or book. Since I'm an author that writes in 4 different genres, I have 4 different media kits I use when I'm on the speaking circuit. The media kit that I present depends upon what set of books people want me to speak about. It is all about doing my best to promote not only myself but also my host's event.

The point of all this is that you want to give your podcaster, event planner, or emcee all the information they need in a digital format so that they can promote you and their event in the simplest and easiest way possible. This is done by giving them all of your information digitally and shareable. Allow them to be able to share that information with all their teams and contractors who are helping them with their podcast or event.

One of the best ways to do that is to use a Google document to share this information. There are many platforms out there that allow you to share digital information, but I prefer Google documents for me and my team. The point is this. Your media kit, no matter the platform you use to share documents, must be:

- Easy to navigate.
- Have active hyperlinks in the shareable document.
- Be accessible as a public file.

One of the biggest time-wasters a podcaster has is in the accessing of information for their guests. Many times, I have guests tell me, "Just look it up on my website. All my information is there." Clearly, this is not a professional guest. Treat a podcaster like that, and you won't be asked back onto the show. The point is you want to make the information your podcaster needs as easily accessible as possible. Don't ask them to dig around 5 pages of your website trying to cut and paste your content and grab your images in a blurred format. Blurred images make the podcaster look unprofessional when they post to their websites and promote to their platforms. It also doesn't show you in your best light either. No one wins with this sort of data exchange.

The media kit that I am going to coach you on gets rave reviews from every podcaster, event planner and organizer to whom I have delivered it. The style of the media kit is not nearly as important as how accessible the information is for the teams of pre- and post-production crews that will be using your kit to create the thumbnails for their show notes, social media announcements, flyers and blog posts. The most frequent comment I've received (as well as my students who have taken my online course for the creation of their media kits) has been, "Wow, your kit is so clean looking." Over and over, my students and I are continually complimented on the cleanliness and professionalism of our media kits. It isn't due to their design. It isn't due to their color choices or use of images. It is due to the ease of use of the document itself and the ability of the podcaster to navigate through the material you are offering.

Start with a Google Document

Start with a Google document or other shareable platform, and build your kit in a way that allows someone who doesn't know you to access all the data points that make you a unique guest.

Now, let's get you started on building your media kit. Here are the necessary sections of your document that need to be incorporated.

Your Header

This is obvious information but sometimes overlooked by my guests. Your media kit needs to have your name on it.

Yes, I know, you would think that I wouldn't need to state that part, but it is required for podcasters. Often the email communication that you are going through with your podcaster as you schedule your interview will have you attaching your media kit to assist them. There have been times I've been given a kit without a name in the file name, so when I tried to transfer it to my pre- and post-production teams, we had to copy the file and try to rename it, or worse, we had to email the guest to rename the file thus stalling our ability to progress on our episode with that guest. Anytime I am stalled on a project, the episode is delayed in our content creation schedule.

Because of these sorts of missteps, that guest was delayed in getting onto our programs because we will put them to the back of the line while we wait on information. Anyone who works in any form of media understands that we all have deadlines. Our listeners have come to rely on our broadcasts and our broadcasting times. I have had listeners email me to let me know that my content was released an hour late according to their phone download tag. Believe it or not, listeners schedule events around broadcasting times. Therefore, if you delay in getting information to some podcasters, they will be forced to meet their broadcasting deadline rather than your launch date for your latest book. Make sense?

In your headline, be sure to put your tagline as well. Here is an example from my podcasting media kit I use with my collaborators in the media:

Janine Bolon

Scientist, Author, Podcaster, Sacred Clown

PHONE: 370.747.3760

EMAIL: Janine@the8gates.com

WEBSITE: The8Gates.com

Table of Contents

Right after the header, make sure to build your Table of Contents with hyperlinks. You want your podcaster to be able to click on any of your Table of Contents headers and have them immediately taken to that page of their document. It is easy to do and in Google documents is done automatically by you choosing header titles rather than writing your entire document in "normal text." If you are still a bit fuzzy on what I'm talking about, no problem. Go to YouTube and type into the search bar:

"how to create clickable table of contents in a google doc."

And you will see a group of videos of people showing you how to do this with your document. (Over the past few years, I've learned how to repair my dryer three times, build my above-ground garden boxes and thread my serger through YouTube videos!) I love YouTube for teaching videos!

When completed, your Table of Contents will look something like this (with your clickable links in blue):

Table of Contents

Headshots

Book Images

Quotes

Bios

Testimonials

Interview Questions

Course Description

Social Media Links

Once you know how to make your Table of Contents clickable, it really builds itself as you create the rest of your media kit. As you continue to add your information to the different sections, just keep in mind that this kit is to speed up the process of promotion for your podcaster. Make things simple and easy for them.

Headshots

When you are posting headshots in your document, make sure:

- They are high quality .jpg or .png files.
- The image isn't blurry.
- There are a variety of looks for you (close-ups, professional poses, etc.).
- There are some pictures of you engaged in your hobbies (swimming, hiking, frisbee, outdoors, etc.).

Unless you are a photographer, I recommend that you get multiple headshots taken by a professional as well as some action shots of you doing the things you love (teaching, hiking, painting, swimming, etc.). It is important that you give your podcaster multiple images so that they can be fitted to the different sizes of banners, backgrounds, thumbnails and social media post requirements they are working under.

Currently, my pre- and post-production teams have 8 different size variants they create. This is required to match thumbnail and banner elements while promoting our guests on 27 different platforms. It is wonderful to have a variety of photos to work with in all the social media we use and post to. It also allows our websites to promote your interests and bring another level of intimacy to your audience through the use of those action shots of you playing with your dog or learning to drive a backhoe.

Book Images

When I started publishing my books in 2005, there were zero free software options available to give your book a 3D image. Most of my books had 2D flat faces, but over the last few years, we are now able to create multiple images for our books and create a variety of images for marketing purposes.

Please be sure to include in your media kit, a 2D image of your book and whatever 3D images of your book you can create or have created for you. This will allow your podcaster to promote your book in a variety of ways. If you haven't found them yet, I highly recommend going to Fiverr - Freelance Services Marketplace for Businesses (**Fiverr.com**) and find a freelance graphic designer who will build what you need for your book cover at a reasonable price. I have now learned how to build these images myself, but if you're short on time, then I would hire someone off of Fiverr to assist you.

Quotes

This is not a necessary section of your media kit, but it sure does help out those podcast hosts who like to build quotable posts for their social media.

I was often surprised how my quotes from my book or my speaking engagements were included in the marketing of the various podcast hosts who had interviewed me. Sometimes it was months after the show had aired and I would see a quote of mine end up on Twitter or LinkedIn. Not only were these hosts quoting my stuff, but they were also making sure to use those gold nuggets to show their listeners that my content was valuable. This makes them look good as well as they are continually supporting their audience with in-depth information.

Be sure to place in this section of your kit those quick 1–2 sentences that you find yourself repeating over and over and over. They can be your favorite tagline, definition of the problem you solve for your clients or how you are referred to by your students and readers. After giving hundreds of lectures and being on so many shows, I have a list of questions in my head that I know people will ask about the content I am sharing. I give those questions to my podcaster because it will make them look super awesome as they are asking me to discuss the topic.

As an author, speaker and teacher, I always want my interviewer to look prepared, well-read, and dynamic. Supplying the podcaster with this sort of information assists them.

Bios

In my media kit, there are three separate bios. They all say the same thing, but they are different lengths to assist my hosts when introducing me.

I've had some podcasters introduce me on my long bio, market my episode with the medium bio and tweet about my guest appearance using my 150-character bio. That's why it is important to include all three in your kit. This is the range of word count that works best for your hosts.

- Long Bio: 300–500 words (roughly two short paragraphs)
- Short Bio: 100–300 words (single paragraph)
- 150–character bio (used for social media platforms with character limitations)

After you have written your bios, take a few minutes and read them out loud.

Please read your bio out loud.

Record yourself reading and listen to the play back. There have been times I've had to totally re-write a guest's bio because I couldn't get my words to come out in a fluid way for their introductions. I want people to see my guests as professional and of high quality. I don't want to appear as if I'm struggling to introduce them. Your introduction should flow in the word choices you've used.

I remember one guest who had so many awards and acronyms in their introduction that I was unable to articulate it in a smooth and valuable way. I ended up asking my guest before we started recording what each of his awards were, how he earned them and what did they mean to people who had never heard of them before? It took us 15 minutes of chatting and another 5 minutes of me rewriting it so that I could bring it all together for him and make the introduction smooth and dynamic for the audience rather than me just rattling off a bunch of titles like so much alphabet soup. Instead, we built a bit of a story around each award in a sentence or two. This made for a longer introduction, but it highlighted my guest better. And that's what I wish for you as well.

Topics of Conversation

In your media kit, it is handy to have 3–4 topics that you would like to talk about to the podcaster's audience. This is the key to making sure that your conversation will be a great fit to the podcaster's audience.

I will go into detail on working these topics out for your media kit later. Just know that this is not just about your book; this is about you as a human being on Planet Earth. All the life experiences, activities and hobbies that you have puttered about in and have been inspired by or written about are open for discussion in an interview.

Testimonials

Having testimonials in your media kit is not required but helpful. When I'm interviewing a guest, I like to refer to how their audience talks about them, using the words from the testimonials. Not only does this help me with introducing my guest, but as a podcaster and book author, I know how much connection it brings together for a community to hear 3rd party references to the speaker and their books and content.

This helps my audience understand that it isn't just me and my guest on this show and that my guest has their own audience, their own content and their own community that listens to and respects what they have to say. It is another way for me to bring in their authority to the podcast. As to the number of testimonials, just pick the top three. What you are showcasing here are the descriptive words people have used to describe you and your message.

Interview Questions

Nobody knows you better than you. With that being said, it is wonderful as a podcaster to have a list of questions that you (the guest & author) want me to ask you so that we can direct our conversation and our listeners into specific aspects of your life, your content and your works in a fun and entertaining way.

Sure, you can have a podcaster ask you the obvious questions that need to be asked about your book, your purpose for writing it and your overall message, but it is also important to throw in a few questions that humanize you and help the host bring in other aspects of your life, such as:

Did you really climb Mount Meeker during a lightning storm? Tell us about that!

What was going on in your life that you decided to enter the National Arm Wrestling competition and won?

Your favorite charity is "Ride2Thrive." Tell us about your involvement and why that is so important to you.

Yes, your book is important. Yes, your content is high quality. However, your personal story is what really matters when you're on a podcast program. Your personality and little details of your life, those hobbies you have and the way you see the world is the perspective that most podcasters are looking for when interviewing you.

Be sure to put in your media kit those sorts of questions as well. Guide your host to places you love and enjoy that aren't necessarily discussed in your book! You are bringing added content to the podcaster's community. They will love you for it (the podcaster and the listeners)!

Course Description

Do you have an online program that you are currently running? Are you getting ready to launch a new program, write another book or have some other offering for the host's audience? Please be sure to put that in your media kit so the host can highlight it during your interview. Toward the end of most podcasts, the host will give you 30–60 seconds to tell their audience where they can go to find out more about you. This is your opportunity to drive traffic into your upcoming course, to attract beta readers for your next book or to get people into your monthly updates. Be sure to put your primary program, course or service you have available into your media kit.

Social Media Links

Ah. Now is the time to discuss the ever-pervasive social media. It is a primary tool in every author's tool kit. Make sure to supply your podcaster with your social media links. I know this sounds so simple, but it is incredibly important. When I first started hosting guests in 2017, I would have people tell me, "Just look me up!" They had no idea that their name would register 9 people—all with the same name. This is the portion of your media kit that is most valuable to the podcaster's post-production teams. The podcaster will have show notes and social media posts where they will tag you or mention you.

Please be sure that you have "friended" and "connected" with the podcaster.

There have been many times where my post-production team has had to reach out to our guests and request that they "friend" or "connect" with me so that we could tag them appropriately on various platforms. This is additional time that we have to put into getting your episode in front of our audience as well as yours.

Be sure to list out your social media with links for your podcaster.

LinkedIn:
LinkedIn.com/in/janinebolon
Facebook:
Facebook.com/janine.bolon
Instagram:
Instagram.com/janinebolon
Pinterest:
Pinterest.com/janinebolon
Twitter:
Twitter.com/janinebolon

Goodreads:
Goodreads.com/user/show/118165246-janine-bolon
DeviantArt:
DeviantArt.com/motherclown

And don't forget to add your website, if you don't have it listed in your header!

Hashtags

We were gifted the use of hashtags in 2007 through the Twitter platform. Since then, there are whole social media marketing strategies built around them and linking your information and content with others of similar interests and passions. If you are one of those authors who wish to have more than their name and book title used in a hashtag, then I suggest you put them down in your media kit so that your host can use them with their post-production promotion and marketing.

Each author has to decide on their own what is best for their work on this one. I just mention it because of how I track my media appearances.

#yourname

#yourbooktitle

#yourbookseries

AFTER THE INTERVIEW

Now that you have completed your podcast interview with your show host, it is time to do the follow-up. I know, I know, it may take several weeks or even months before your show goes up on your podcaster's platform, but today you need to write them a thank you note and pop it into the mail for them. Ask them for their address before you get off your interview, and let them know that you're "old school" and you still send thank you notes.

Just by asking them for their address to send a thank you note puts you leagues ahead of all their other guests! Less than 1% of guests send follow-up thank you emails, much less *a note in the mail.*

Sending a follow-up thank you note puts you heads-and-shoulders above the crowd. Basically, your media kit demonstrates you are a professional. Your preparation for the podcast shows your ability. The thank you card in the mail makes you a STAR!

Your Social Media

Once you've finished recording the show with your podcaster and you've sent your thank you note, then the next step is to get onto your social media platform and let folks know you've just recorded a show with the podcaster.

Find the podcaster's logo for the show, the website the show resides on or a link to the show's Spotify®, YouTube or iTunes channel and basically give your audience a preview of the person, the show and the channel. These are the types of questions you ask your host after you've done the interview:

Hey [Podcast Host Name]

Thank you so much for having me on your show. There are a few questions I have for you before we sign off today:

What is your mailing address?

What logo do you wish me to use?

What platform do you wish me to promote? Your website, Spotify, iTunes, YouTube?

Explain to the host that you want to let your audience know of your coming episode and you wish to have your promotional details in place. The host will love you for this!

Promoting the Show

Now that you have the details of how best to promote the host's show, get on your social media or newsletter and cue up a mention of your episode, what topic you discussed and one or two of the points you made on the show. Give your audience a reason to listen to this episode.

Then, when your episode goes live and is available to your audience, you do this all again with the social media and newsletter to give your audience an opportunity to hear all about it.

People are busy. You are busy. Your host is busy. Give your audience a second chance to learn about your interview, your host's show, and the quality content that you are delivering for free to them. Everyone wins with podcasting!

Follow Up with the Show Host

Your episode is now available to your audience. You've sent out Facebook, LinkedIn and your newsletter messages to let your communities know about the episode. You've thanked your host with a thank you letter and by promoting the show to your people. Please make sure that you are friends or connected to the show host so that you can tag them on the platforms and they see that you are mentioning them and their show.

Once you have done all this for your episode, the last item to put into place is to follow up with your podcaster in a few months' time. Put it down in your calendar or on your reminders to follow up with each and every podcaster you've been interviewed by to be on their show again. Not only ask them to be on the show again, but also see if there is a different direction they wish to go with the original content or if they want a fresh perspective on content they are promoting on their show.

This is the co-creative process at its best. Some of the most fun I've had is where a podcast host and I created a show for both of our audiences where we were able to give 15 tips in an hour-long show. We ended up writing a book chapter together and went on to do a 15-step online email course for our audience and our different communities. I'm not saying every host will be wanting you back, but why not follow up with the folks who have already had you on the show? This makes the process much smoother.

I've also had more than one host request that I follow up with them in a year because they have themes of their shows. Be sure to have a follow-up system that you use to make these appointments for yourself! Follow-up is key.

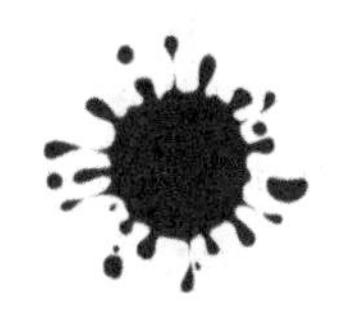

TAKING YOUR BOOK ON TOUR

If you're an author like me, you may not have listened to many podcasts. Audiobooks may not be something you do unless you're traveling in your car. For me, I was such a busy mother homeschooling my four children, writing books between the hours of 4am–6am, running a business and keeping up with my online students, podcasting wasn't an activity that I felt I had the mental space to do.

However, as my children got older and as I managed to find more and more time where I had space to myself (i.e., I had times where no one was talking to me.), I started to find an appreciation for audiobooks and podcasts that I didn't have before. It doesn't matter if you're a podcast listener or even an avid fan of them. You can still make use of podcasts and be a valued guest for the communities that have been built by the podcast hosts. Here is a simplified outline of activities that will assist you in preparing your book for an audio tour.

Time to Make a List

First of all, write down the areas that your book covers or the genre of your fictional work. Make a list of all the topics you could talk about regarding your book, its stories, characters and environments. Then, add to that list all of the hobbies, activities and topics you could talk about. When I first did this exercise for myself, I was stunned that I had two pages worth of topics I could talk about.

You and I both know that you are more than your book. You have a life outside of your book, and listeners want to learn more about the "real" you, not just the "author" you. Right? So, figure out the areas of your life you don't mind sharing. The fun stuff you do is of interest to the listeners (things like camping with your kids, scuba diving, working with girl scouts or learning Cajun cooking). Whatever you are doing outside of writing is wonderful content and material for your podcast host to work with. One of my topics that I share with podcasters is that I was struck by lightning when I was in elementary school. This event spawned a whole series of books I've written.

So, take the time to write up a list of things you can speak about. You don't have to be an expert in any of these areas. The point is you have experiences in them, and you can speak about them in an entertaining way. I have stories of when I used to go scuba diving with my dad and how he would teach me to buddy breathe with one regulator as well as how to avoid the dangerous fish that had poisonous bites. You have a lifetime of experiences to pull out of your mental hat right now. Make a list of the things that you've had fun doing and share those with your audience.

Pick Your Top Three Topics

Now that you have a list of life experiences and activities that you can speak about, it is time to pick your top 3–4 topics that you will put into your media kit as discussions you can have with your podcast host. It is a lot of fun to use a snappy title for these topics so that your host can see that you don't take yourself or your book too seriously. It allows your sense of humor to come through, and you'll find large groups of people that love the way you talk as well as your perspective of the world.

Some examples I've used over the years:

The Peloponnesian War: What can I Learn from a Bunch of Old, Dead, Greek Guys?

Money, It's Not Just for Rich People!

Don't Just Do Something, Sit There: 3 Minute Meditations for the Overwhelmed!

The purpose of your topic title is to give your audience an opportunity to know your quirky, fun-loving side. You see the world differently from other people. (Face the fact that we authors are quirky by the sheer nature of our craft, right? Who else looks up 15 different ways a human can die from natural poisons? Okay, maybe you aren't a mystery writer, but you get my point.) Don't be afraid to trot out your humor for your titles. By not taking yourself too seriously, you lighten up, and people want to get to know you better because of the perspective you present to their world.

Gather Podcasts

You now have a huge list of topics you can speak on. You have titles for your top three talks you can give to podcast hosts and event planners. It is now time for you to get a spreadsheet pulled up on your computer and call it:

"My Audio Book Tour"

I recommend that you name the columns in the following order for ease of use:

Column A: Podcast Name

Column B: Contact Name

Column C. Website (or contact mode)

Column D: Initially Contacted (date)
Column E: Follow Up (date)
Column F: Notes/Plan/Response
Column G. Address (email or physical address)
Column H: Book Sent (digitally or physical book)
Column I: Thank You Note Sent

When I first started doing podcasting tours in 2015, the show hosts were always so surprised to hear from a self-published author and were more than happy to chat with me about being a guest. Now, we have a bunch more podcasters in the world, and it is even easier to get onto shows! What is wonderful about podcasting and audio tours is the fact that you'll get into audiences and communities that you would never dream of seeking out any other way. One of my biggest surprises was a Professional Pool Cleaner's Podcast Program that had me on as an author giving advice to their membership on how to increase their business by calling clients and checking up on them. This was during the height of the pandemic, and all I did was see their request for guests on Facebook and offered to be on their show.

For you and your book, I recommend that you create your spreadsheet because as you get on more and more shows, you're going to need to have all this information in one place so that as you tour, you'll always have this information at hand. The first several columns that you are filling out for the shows' contact information, etc., is simple enough to understand, but let's discuss Column F–I.

Column F: is listed as Notes/Plan/Response, the section that I list out any notes or requests the host has for me as the guest. I also use this space to remind myself if I've sent my media kit to the host already or if I need to add or delete anything from my media kit. I've had some hosts request only a single headshot and a short bio. This is the column I put that sort of information. I don't assume I will be able to find the email that lists all of this out, so I make sure to place any special requests from hosts here.

Column G: is the physical address or the email address of the primary contact person I need to communicate with. Since I like to send thank you cards to my hosts as well as send them copies of my book, I make sure that I have mailing addresses as well as email addresses listed out on my spreadsheet.

Column H: is a reminder to me that the book has been mailed or emailed to the host for reference. Some hosts read it, others do not. Some podcast hosts are so busy they only have 5–10 minutes before the show to read over your bio and interview you. The point is you want to make sure you give the host as much information as needed and not to overwhelm them before your interview. Your contact for the podcast show will let you know what is required, and then you can send along your book as a thank you along with a note if that seems appropriate.

Column I: is again, a reminder to me that I have sent along a "thank you" note to the host for having me on their show. This earns me more positive mention points than anything else I do for my podcasting hosts. I've reached back around to hosts years after our interviews and they still remember me because of those little "thank you" cards I send them in the mail. I highly recommend you obtain mailing addresses from all your hosts and send them cards. You'll get a lot more promotion for your time!

After you have created your spreadsheet, it is now time to start contacting podcasters and asking them if you may be a guest on their show. Here are some suggestions for how to do that.

Finding Podcasts Through Readers & Colleagues

As an author, I know you have an email list of subscribers who enjoy hearing from you. Now is the time for you to contact them in your next newsletter and ask them what their favorite podcasts are. Let them know that you wish to be a guest on podcasts and you would like to chat with the hosts of their favorite programs.

I've been surprised how many people responded to my request. With that meager beginning, I now have a large network of friends and colleagues who are all podcast hosts and wish to have me on their programs. I loved podcasts because I didn't have to worry about the video and what I looked like. I would just get on a phone call or zoom meeting with a host and we would record our conversations. It just seemed more fun and relaxing for me.

After you reach out to your newsletter subscribers, I would ask all the colleagues you have if they have a podcast show and if you would be a good fit for their audience. By having your top 3 topics already lined up as well as your list of hobbies and interests that you can speak about, do you see how you are primed and ready to be a podcast guest? You know exactly if you are a good fit or not. In the 21 years that I have been actively on the audio tour circuit with my books, I have only had a handful of podcasts where the host and I knew immediately that I was not a good fit for their listeners. What has always amazed me was how quick those handful of hosts quickly recommended their buddies' shows to me. So even if you get a "no" answer, you may get a referral for another podcast. A referral is awesome.

The wonderful thing about audio tours is you can grow them as fast or as slow as you want. In my career, I've had times where I scheduled one podcast a month to be a guest and other times where I was on shows 2–3 times a week depending on what I was trying to accomplish with my marketing campaigns. The best part of being on an audio tour is you can pace it according to your lifestyle and personality.

Finding Podcasts Through iTunes & Spotify

After you've spoken with your readers and your colleagues about getting on their favorite podcast programs, it is time to seek out podcasts on iTunes & Spotify. This is where you are going to go through your list of hobbies and your talk topics and search through these two platforms to see how many podcasts are being broadcast through those platforms that are in alignment for your book's message.

After you've done your searches through the podcasts and have found 8–10 programs that look promising for you, start listening to one of the shows from each podcast. Take notes and then you can email the podcaster a message similar to this:

Hi, [Podcast Host].

I just finished listening to your podcast called, [Name of podcast episode]. I really liked the points you made on [list the items you took away from the episode from your notes]. It really helped me understand the topic better.

Because of your topic on [pick one that fits with your book's message], I thought I could be an appropriate guest for your podcast. Are you accepting guests for your show right now?

I've just written a book called, [Title of your book] that discusses something similar to your episode on [put the episodes main focus here], and it correlates to the issues my book solves.

Is there any chance we can get on a quick phone call or zoom to see if my message is a good fit for your listeners?

You can reach me:

Phone number:

LinkedIn profile page:

I look forward to hearing from you,

[Your Name]

Send your email to the show's host, and then follow up with the host in 2 weeks (if they haven't responded to you) with this email:

Hi there, [Host's Name].

I wanted to bring this email back up to the top of your inbox. I know how busy life can get.

I look forward to chatting with you,

[Your Name]

And keep following up with your podcasters every 2 weeks until they tell you they don't have a space for you or you hear back from them. This system has worked well for me, and I usually get an answer from most of my podcasters at that 2–4-week mark.

The point to all this is to get into as many podcast programs as your lifestyle will allow. And the more podcasters you communicate with, the more shows you will be asked to be on.

And don't forget to ask me if you can be my guest. Let me know you've read this book, and we'll be sure to get you on our program, *The Writer's Hour Creative Conversations.*

CASE STUDY #1: CHRIS RIEDEL & BLOOD MONEY

This is an interview I did in May 2021, where I asked several of my students who took my "Media Kit Course" to share with you what helped and how they benefited from the course in getting their books promoted through podcasting. Chris Riedel was an author who was referred to me by a fellow podcaster. Because I require a media kit for all my guests, Chris took my course and then agreed to have me interview him on the results. Here is our discussion:

Janine: Today I am with Chris Niedel, author of the book, *Blood Money: One Man's Bare-Knuckle Fight to Protect Taxpayers from Medical Fraud.* Welcome Chris! Let's just jump right in. As an author, you decided to write a book on something you are absolutely passionate about, saving taxpayers millions of dollars for the state of California. One of the things that probably came as a surprise for you was the simple fact of, "Well the book is done, now the real marketing starts." With that, tell me a little bit about how you chose to market your book, originally.

Chris Riedel: I have learned all of the horror stories about trying to find an agent from the publisher are true. The only thing that gave me comfort was that John Grisham was turned down 30 times on his first book, which of course, was a bestseller.

I spent months trying to find an agent, and I got nothing but rejects. "We are not doing this right now; we are going to write journals." I gave up on that. Then I decided that I would self-publish or combination-publish, but I was introduced to Acorn. I really liked Acorn, so I hired them to publish the book. But now I gotta sell it. I do not know how to sell books.

Janine: It makes you almost want to scream at the world, "Hey! I am an author, not a marketing geek!" Right?

Chris: Yes. I got some wonderful information from you on your website. Wonderful. Then I asked the publisher if she could recommend a marketing person, and she did. She recommended someone who can do the audio for it, and she did. They have been doing the marketing, but it has not been nearly as extensive as I would like. I am sitting here, pondering, "How do I do podcasts? How do I do this?" So, your book is going to be perfect for me.

Janine: Right. One of the things that was new for you was when I asked you for a media kit and you were like, "A what?" So, if you do not mind, talk about your process of learning what a media kit was because you had multiple resources, not just me on that one.

Chris: Yeah, I did, and I was working with an established author who had never heard of a media kit like you suggested. He just put out a bunch of web pictures and whatnot. And I loved the way it was organized; anybody could click on a subject matter and immediately go right to what they were interested in. That was fantastic.

Janine: One of the things that I will be talking about in the book is how to be a podcaster's best guest ever. When you do that, you are invited over and over again. If you are an author and you know you are going to be a multi-book author, you want to hang on to all the podcast people that you have been a part of. You want to hang on to those contacts because when you get ready to launch your next book, then you are ready to go on that virtual book tour. This is what 2020 taught us, that the ways of doing the old book tours are out; they are gone until people open back up. Even then, you are just not going to be able to have the impact that you can say on a podcast, which is evergreen. It will always be out there for you to be able to access and send your people to.

When it came to a media kit, what was the idea that you had, and how did you decide to put it together for your book because you are contemplating writing yet another book? With that second book in your mind rumbling around in there, how will you write the book and then cater the media kit for your virtual book tour that you will do next time?

Chris: What my kits taught me as an author that helped me is that you should have a website. You have got a nice website; they will figure it out. What your media kit does is it adds a specific place that podcast users or others can go and click on, and it is exactly what it will be. It will take them right there, and it is like, "Dude, this sure makes a lot of sense."

Janine: It saves podcasters a lot of time too, right? You want to help them save time because when you do your follow-up, your little thank you card or thank you email or whatever, you want them to invite you back because you worked hard to get a spot on that podcast show, whoever it was that you were with.

What is your experience with the various podcasting elements? What have been some of the good aspects for it, for you?

Chris: Actually, I have had triple podcasts, and I have really enjoyed it. The hosts were very nice, and they were very experienced like you. I got right into it. I enjoy it. I am trying to figure out now, how do I get a whole bunch more interviews like this? That is how you market today.

Janine: Let's chat a bit about what you do after your podcast episode has been broadcast. The best thing to do is after your podcast has gone live is you have written your thank you note to the host and then you share your episode in all your social media as well as your newsletter to your readers. It is always a good thing to send an email back to the podcaster saying, "Hey, this is how I highlighted your show. I hope you get more listeners." Right? That is what the podcaster wants, more listeners, that way we get sponsors, and of course, you want more people to listen so that they hear about your book.

The next thing you do is another follow-up, about 4 to 6 weeks after your podcast has gone live, and you ask, "Hi. Do you have any openings for the next season?" That is question number 1. "We can talk about the different aspects," depending upon what you talked about with that podcaster. Offer up different areas that you can talk about for them. The second thing is, "If you do not have any openings for your next season, do you know of any other podcasters who are looking for guests like myself?" Ask for the referral. This is Sales 101, Marketing 101. However, that is what people forget all the time. I have had over 52 people who have been a guest on my shows and not one has asked me for a referral to another podcaster yet.

Chris: That does save time.

Janine: This is something most people are not doing, promoting the shows they've been on and then following up with the podcaster to let them know how you've promoted their show, and finally, asking for the referral. As you know in sales, where is the fortune? The fortune is in the follow-up. That is where I am going to really encourage in the book is that everybody follow up. The first one is you thank them, then you follow up with them, then you show them how you have promoted their show. They always appreciate that. The third one is to ask for the referral, ask for other podcasters, because podcasters collaborate with each other all the time. They form their own networks.

As you move forward with your virtual book tour, if you will, another idea is to call local radio stations. Radio is not dead, as a lot of people like to think it is. They think it is all online and satellite radio. The thing is, you call local radio stations and ask them when they have their talk shows, and do they have a book review, or do they have time for that. And they will definitely connect you. Talk radio is always looking for guests.

That is where your media kit will make you look so professional. "Here is my media kit. Can I fit into any of your time slots? I would love to help out your listeners. What do you talk about?" It is very active in the Midwest because you have a lot of people that are working on farms and that sort of thing, and they continue to listen to the radio. Those are some ideas for you, Chris, to help you get more promotional time.

Janine: Anything else I can help you out with, Chris? Any other ideas for your virtual book tour?

Chris: This is definitely a lot.

Janine: Okay. I will stop the recording.

CASE STUDY #2: JADE ALEXANDER & VIDEO MEDIA KITS

This is an interview with Jade Alexander from Synergistic Videography in March 2021.

Janine: I would just want to chat a little bit about the media kit. One of the things that is very true for you, Jade, is that you are an incredibly adept videographer. You have been in the media. You have done Hollywood. You have done so many different types of video expressions for people. You have worked with artists. You have worked with creatives. You have worked with very serious business owners and TEDx speakers. You have a lot of experience, but at the same time, you still took my media kit course for podcasting. I would love to learn from you why it was helpful and then the areas where it was very different from what you need when you get into videography and the video media.

Jade Alexander: Your class is really great. I mean, of course, when you have taken a lot of classes that are in the same vein, there are some repetitive things, but there are very few and far between. The reason I say that is: One of the things that you did with your media kit that most people do not teach was the variety of media kits you need depending on where you are. Most people, especially when they say (I am sure you have heard this), "I am a speaker. I am an author. I am a blah blah blah. I raised seahorses." Whatever, right? They have that whole plethora of things that they do, but they only have one media kit. Really reinforcing that authors need a different media kit than those that are speakers and those that are on podcasts. They all are slightly different. Having those available is really important.

Of course, some things crossover, but you gave great examples of yourself because you are a, what do you call yourself? A serial solopreneur? Is that the term you use? You have all these other things. You have those examples of variety, and you have downloadable content. This is the first media kit class that I have taken that actually has files to download that you can literally play and plug. That you do not have to reinvent the wheel. That was super helpful.

Second thing I really liked that I have not seen in any other course was the Table of Contents. A lot of us are just accustomed to scrolling through. When I did my original media kit, I did separate folders on Google Drive because I found that to be easier as far as organization. But my one-sheet was not like that. It was a scroll down with the Table of Contents in there as a hotlink, not just like, "Here. Go to page seven." Then they have to scroll to page seven to literally click on that and get there. That was absolutely essential, I think, for organization. It really reflects your professionalism. To have it all in one place, whether you are really organized in your real life, your day-to-day life, or not. The fact that you are showing that you can be, that you are prompt and it is ready to go, is so critical.

I have talked to a lot of media planners and people that are like, "Yeah, this person is really famous. They have been on this many TEDx things." But when I got their media kit, girl, you have no idea what it looks like. It was awful. If you are new to the speaking world, it is going to be super important to have a really organized media kit. They have so many fish in the sea to choose from. If yours is not put together, if it is not easy to understand, if your links are broken or whatever, they might just move on and most likely they will. Because it is their time that they are spending on you. So, make it worth every second. I just loved how you did that.

Janine: Well, thank you. Let's define a bit more about what you mean when it comes to a speaker one -sheet. I talked about it a little bit in the course, but I think it is helpful to hear it from a videographer. I am coming to the topic as a podcaster and radio show host because that is my strong suit. But for you as a videographer, talk to us about what it means to have a speaker one-sheet for folks who are after the keynote addresses, speaking at events and working with event planners.

Jade: That is a great question. When it comes to the one-sheet, let us say that I come to your speaking event. I record your thirty minutes, half-hour, seventy hours, whatever happens to be video. I have the raw files from there. But for me to make a nice, beautiful speaker reel or sizzle reel or record the whole speaking event, you can section it out and sell it. Whatever it happens to be. I need some basic components to make sure that your brand is built in.

We want to have your brand on every single thing. So, I need to know things like, what colors do you like to use? What fonts do you prefer? I need your headshot in certain sizes. I need to have your logo in a vector. If you do not know what a vector is, it is basically a logo that has no background. Because I am going to put that in the bottom right-hand corner of your video. I am going to have it look like a watermark. It is kind of grayed out a little bit. It is not as vibrant so it does not distract. But that branding is there.

The last thing I always have to ask speakers for is their contact information. If you have this big, beautiful video and there is no way to contact you at the end, your video is doing you a disservice. People are not only frustrated like, "Well, she had all this other stuff together. What happened to this?" So, I need that contact information. A lot of people's one-sheets, they have it all put together for me. They have their contact information, their hashtags, their credentials, all those things.

So, when I pop up at the bottom of the title and text, this is what we call it, when you first get on stage. We cannot always include on the videos the MC where they are saying all these great things about you. Usually, where we start the filming is after people are done clapping and you are right into your talk. We will put a bottom third. Kind of like what you see on the news where it is the anchor's name and then their credentials. We will put, "Janine Bolon, author, speaker, renowned for blah." Whatever that happens to be, I need to know what that is. I am going to copy and paste it out of your one-sheet. I am not going to allow any kind of mistakes on that. So, make sure that it is spelled correctly as well.

Janine: These are just some of the basics of what it means to have a media kit. Depending upon your venue, event, or what the media format is that you are moving into, your media kit needs to change as we talked about before. Is there anything else you would care to share with the reader?

Jade: I think the main thing that I like to share with people is something that I teach in my courses for speakers, which is when you have videos of you previously doing a talk or video testimonials, when you have those hyperlinks in your one-sheet or in your Google Drive folder—whatever it happens to be—do it one of two ways. Have the hyperlink, and make sure you can take care of that hyperlink. Meaning, that it is on your YouTube channel or your website. So, it is never broken. It always goes to the right place. Nothing is more unprofessional than to have this great video that you paid all this money for and they click on it and it does not go anywhere. So, make sure that you own whatever location it is in.

The second thing I like to tell speakers is that if you have a sizzle reel or if you have some type of video that you need to play at the beginning or end of your talk, put that in your media kit. Put it in that file that you are sending them as far as that Google Drive file. Make it very clearly labeled with your name. Make sure it is an mp4, SD, and HD because you do not know on the venue what size of screen they are going to use. If it is too big of a screen and you sent them a small file, it is going to look bad. If the file is too big it will not play right. So, give them all those file options.

That way, you can just send that link to the AV guys because what they are going to do is grab their laptops. They would be like, "Okay. Email me the video." You are going to have the real file as well as the hyperlinks. Why do I tell you to have the real file? Because some hotels' Wi-Fi may not be fast enough, or maybe they did not pay for the Wi-Fi because event planners have to pay for that. It may not be connected. You need to have the real file for them to download and play. Just make it easier on them. Because if they love you, they tell event planners. If they do not like you, they will say everything about how bad you were. The event planners then pass that along. So do as much as you can do to help the AV people out. We are your best friends in the back. Believe it or not. Have it available to us in multiple formats. That way we can make sure you look good. That would be the last thing I would say.

Janine: Thanks so much, Jade. I appreciate your time today.

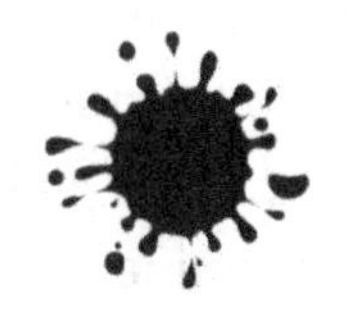

CASE STUDY #3: MEREDITH BELL & TEACHER, THEN AUTHOR

This is an interview with Meredith Bell. President of Performance Support Systems.

Janine: Hello, and welcome to your bonus feature for *Author Podcasting*. Thank you for joining us, and I wanted to share with you, author, businesswoman and coach, Meredith Bell. Something the readers and listeners will want to know is that Meredith and I are both authors, multi-genre, meaning multiple books. We both have been businesswomen for almost all of our lives. We are both podcasters, and we both came to podcasting from very different routes but with similar goals in mind. And so, this is something that I thought was perfect for you as an author. So, you can see not only both sides, but we have also been guests, we have been hosts, and we are going to share a little bit of our experiences. Meredith, thank you so much for taking the time to do this today.

Meredith Bell: Oh, I am delighted to have this conversation with you Janine.

Janine: And I would love for you to introduce yourself a little bit. Talk about where you came from as a corporate woman, how you became a business-woman, and then talk to us about the books that you write. We'd love to hear a little history about you.

Meredith: Okay, I came from education, not corporate. I was a teacher and then in a supervisory managerial role and realized I do not do politics or bureaucracy. And so, I left, and this should be an encouragement to any of your listeners who are considering leaving. I had never had a course in business. I really did not know what I was doing, but I just knew I was miserable where I was, and the unknown had to be better than that. My favorite thing was communication skills, helping teachers learn how to interact more effectively with their students and with each other.

And so that is what I focused my business on. I was initially helping small business owners and then different sizes of organizations by doing leadership development team building, and the core underlying theme of everything was helping people learn how to interact more effectively together. That was my driving force, and I did that on my own for a number of years and then met my two business partners. And we have been working together now for 30 years. We no longer do the consulting and training. We are a software company and book publisher. So, our focus has not changed. We still want to help people interact more effectively with each other in the workplace.

And so, I wrote my first book by myself, *Strong for Performance* in early 2020, and launched it right around the time of the pandemic. And I thought, "You know what? I am just going for it anyway." And I was able to draw on support from people who have known me over the years. And that was all about what it takes to really make your training program stick and create a culture of coaching where people support each other. And then Denny Coates (my business partner) and I decided to pull our 30-some years of knowledge around interpersonal skills together in the book, Connect with Your Team: Mastering the Top 10 Communication Skills.

And so, that is the big book that I have been really getting booked on podcasts as a guest around because we also created a companion book, Peer Coaching Made Simple, to help people partner up with somebody when they are trying to improve their communication skills. And our goal because we know how painful and really unnecessary pain that is in the workplace around the lack of effective, communication and interactions. We want to sell a million copies of these books. We feel it's that important.

Janine: Correct. And one of the things that first impressed me about you was that you did not make any bones about it; you let me know that was your goal. And I was like, "Okay, let me see what I can do to help you sell a million copies because relationships go down the tubes." Personal relationships go down the tubes with communication, and we hear about it a lot of times. But when it comes to brass tacks, okay, how do I go about making these changes? And that's the thing that I really enjoyed not only about your book but also about how many of your podcast interviews that you and I have had together have been. You have these 10 steps, and then you give these little gold nuggets on your podcast that people can digest and chew and integrate into their own lives whether they are dealing with the business team or personal relationship. It does not matter at all; it applies. Okay. So here you are launching this book in the middle of a pandemic. Hello. Does landscape totally change? Podcasting became the big thing to do virtual book tours through podcasting. So, talk about what you had to learn as a guest to move forward into the podcasting world. How did you do that?

Meredith: Well, I think a key aspect is first knowing who you want your listeners to be. Because that is going to determine which podcast. And actually, I had been a guest on podcasts in the past. Around some of these same areas, just not having had the book to talk about as a part of it. So, I had experienced it as a guest, but what I wanted to do was refine it. And your course actually helped me prepare the marketing side because one of the things that it really helped me do was narrow in on who I am talking to. When I prepare this bio and the questions I want them to ask, will these be relevant for their listeners, for the listeners I want to reach? So that was one of the things that it was worth taking to the time to slow down before I started jumping out and reaching out to a lot of people was really thinking that through. So, becoming more `strategic is a key thing.

And the other thing I often do is I just ask myself before I contact a specific host, "How can I serve them first?" I ask them that before I ask them to have me as a guest on their podcast, and sometimes it is because one of the things I pride myself on is building a big network of people that I form meaningful relationships with. Not just superficial. And so, I have other people that I know that would be great guests on a show. So sometimes I will reach out and say, "I have been listening to your podcast." Oh, another thing is I listen to their podcast to get a sense of their style and if I would be a good fit with their approach, their personality even. Just listen to how they interact with their guests and what kinds of guests they seem to be looking for. So, I make sure I do that before I ever approached the hosts. So, they know I am not just randomly reaching out to dozens or hundreds of hosts. I have chosen them specifically and for a specific reason. And so, I will just include, “I would love to learn more about your ideal guest in case I know people who might be a good match for you, and I might be myself.” So, I will put in a little plug[?] for me but not pushing me as being necessarily the right fit for them. I do not want to make assumptions.

Janine: That is so helpful as a host who runs four different programs that operate on four different demographics. When you approached me about the media kit and you had very specifically told me exactly who you were going for and that you wanted a million copies sold and blah blah, blah, I said, "Okay. I know exactly what show to put you in and that you are appropriate for." And my favorite part as a host is then saying, "Hey, I have had a great guest here." And then this is the other thing you did for me; when I gave you the links to the podcast, you then promoted me and the show on your own network. Now, sometimes guests forget to do that, and like, look, I am trying to expand my reach. That is what helps me with my sponsors. I get more sponsors. I get more people who are interested in servicing this podcast when I have that happen. And so that was one of the things that I was grateful for as a host. So that was something you did for me, okay?

So those are some of the things that you do. Listen to the podcast, and make sure you have a media kit. I offer a media kit course just because I am very specific on what I need from my people. But then the other thing that was helpful is the fact that you are also a podcaster yourself. So, tell us a little bit about your show and what prompted you to run that show.

Meredith: Well, I have been running it since June of 2019. In fact, I just recorded episode 100 this week because I do one per week. I record typically one a week and then release one per week. And just because I wanted to a few years ago, I interviewed some authors about their books because I am just so fanatical about getting good content out to the world if I have read a book that I really like. It was sort of a podcast without formally being one. And then I just decided. You know what? It is time for me to launch one myself because I love asking questions, interviewing people, learning myself, and being able to share wisdom from other people to the world. But also, I have been working because we are a software company, and we have had hundreds of consultants and coaches over the years who have worked with us.

And I knew a lot. Of course, I had been one myself. So, I knew a lot of the things they were challenged with from a marketing and sales perspective or limiting beliefs. And I thought, I really want to serve those people. So that was my initial audience, and I think this is an important thing for people on either side of the microphone; the focus can change. As your podcast grows, the audience can expand. So, I ended up reaching small business owners, leaders, and organizations. And I really have discovered my passion has somewhat changed. I still love coaches and consultants, but I really want to deliver more around the title of my podcast, which is "Strong for Performance." So how can people develop themselves so that they bring their A-game every day whether it is to their work if they are in a job or if they are a business owner? That is really what I am excited about the most.

And that still interests and drives me, and it has caused me to expand who I am considering as my guests. The other thing, Janine, that I will just say for your listeners, for anyone who hesitates to reach out to somebody thinking: "Oh, their show is too big." Or "They are in a position they would not be interested in." Get rid of those thoughts because you would be amazed at how many people want your specific expertise, and if we convince ourselves in advance that they will not want to talk to us, we shoot ourselves in the foot before we have the courage to reach out and ask. The worst they can say is "No." And we are not on their show right now, anyway. If we reach out to ask someone on either side of the mic, it is amazing how many yeses you will get.

Janine: Right. And some people are very flattered. And a lot of times when I have received noes as an author that I am working on getting other podcaster is because the podcaster was wrapping things up. It was because "Oh, I am moving on to other projects." Or stuff like that. Or I had one person say, "I am sorry. It is just not a good fit at all." So, we want that. We want to make sure that where we are is in the right demographic. And we are on that good place. So, there are a lot of resources out there now that were not available when you and I first started podcasting. I started my first radio show in 1996 and my first podcast in 2017, and so you and I have been in this game for a while. And one of the things that I really wanted to share with people is we all have stories about the worst guests. I always like to focus on the worst guests because people will be like, "Oh my gosh, I would never do that." I am like, "Good for you. That's what you need to focus on." When you present yourself to a podcaster is that you would never do these things. So, if you do not mind sharing a few things and then we are going to talk about a wonderful achievement that you have had just this week. But first, I want to talk about the guest that you were just like, "Oh my goodness, I cannot believe this."

Meredith: I think a key thing that I forgot to ask initially of people is have they ever been on a podcast before or how many podcasts have they been on? And I really enjoyed this person as a person in our initial conversation. But she was so uncomfortable just having a conversation that she had to prepare this script in advance and pretty much read from it during the interview. She over-prepared. She was not giving herself enough credit for just knowing her stuff and being able to talk off the cuff. And we discussed it before we did the interview, and I thought, "Well, I have never done this." But she had sent me her questions. It took more time than it really needed to for both of us because she sent me her questions. She also sent me her answers. She even sent me places where she wanted me to insert comments. It was just way more formalized and scripted than I really like to have. And so, I think for your listeners to keep in mind that the host is having you on the show because they have confidence that you know your stuff. Just relax into that. It is unlikely they are going to throw a question at you that you cannot handle because they want you to look good and because they also want to look good. So, I think I am doing a better job of screening people, just from the perspective of finding out how comfortable you are talking off the cuff about your particular area of expertise.

Janine: And one of the things I wanted to share with everyone was, Meredith Bell, as of yesterday or a couple of days ago, I saw posted on LinkedIn where she had interviewed two guests at the same time, and that is quite an accomplishment. As a podcaster, it is one thing to have these wonderful conversations like this. But I have been on podcasts where I have been the host, and I have had five people in only one hour. You are trying to make sure. And so, I understand how you have to pivot pretty quickly with that. I just wanted to say congratulations on that, and talk to us a little bit about what that was like to be a host when you had two guests.

Meredith: Well, it was actually the idea of our good friend, Tom Perone, because he knew, well, I knew too. Walt Hampton is a coach, and Joe Perone, Tom's nephew, is a coach being coached by Walt. Tom was saying, "Wow. I think it would be great if they could talk about their relationship and what it's like to work together." I said, "Yeah, I can do that." Because I know both of them, and I just felt confident in my ability to facilitate. I just prepared some draft questions from the coach's perspective and the coachee's perspective and let them know in advance what the framework would be but that it was going to be, again, a natural conversation, and we would just naturally flow with it. And it worked beautifully because they both had, I think, really valuable things to say.

Janine: I think it works lovely as well. So yeah, I just was very proud of you because I know what it takes to do stuff like that. It takes a lot of preparation, and a lot of times guests do not understand the reason why a show sounds so good. The reason why a show seems to be seamless is because of the amount of preparation the host has to do in advance. So, anything else you would care to share with our authors regarding podcasting that maybe we have not talked about or that popped in your head?

Meredith: Yes, I would like to say that in addition to listening to a couple of episodes, getting a sense of what is important to that host goes a long way to really establish relationships. Because I am not trying typically to get on a show just to be a guest. I want to form a relationship and be of service to that host in the future as well if possible. And so, I think taking the time to get to know them, looking at their LinkedIn profile or wherever they are on social media, or their page about their radio show or podcast. All of that makes a really positive impression because hardly anybody does that. So, if you want to stand out, do those little things. And Janine, you are such an exemplary person at this is writing notes. Thank you notes afterwards and promoting the show, as you mentioned, even before you are on as a guest to let them know. I am really looking forward to being a guest on this person's podcast. So, it alerts people in your sphere about this podcast and helps spread the word about it. The hosts really appreciate that.

Janine: Yes, we all do very much. We appreciate the extra publicity because it serves everyone well, especially in regards to relationship management, which you and I are both into. We want to be able to be successful people, but we want to do that because we cultivate really solid relationships with our people. So, Meredith, thank you so much for being with us today. I really appreciate it, and I am going to close it out now and just let folks know, feel free to work through the transcript that is below and there are going to be links. Not only to Meredith's podcast, Media Kit but also to her website so that you can get to know her a little bit better. I recommend it especially if you have a team of people that you are working with and you want to increase your communication skills. This is Janine Bolon with *Author Podcasting*. Have a great day.

THE MEDIA KIT CHECKLIST

Below you will find the Media Kit Checklist that is available for free on my website.

AuthorPodcasting.com/free

I've reproduced it for you here so you can see how much of the material you need to build your media kit is already within your possession. Most media kits take less than an hour to build out using the tips in this book. Just make sure that your digital kit is easily shareable and editable by your podcast show hosts and their production teams.

Images

- ☐ Headshot—Action
- ☐ Large Headshot
- ☐ Small Headshot

- ☐ Square Book—300x300
- ☐ 3D Book
- ☐ Book—Front Cover—Back Cover

Content

- ☐ Bio—Long
- ☐ Bio—Short
- ☐ Bio—150 characters
- ☐ Book Description—Summary
- ☐ Book Description—Short Blurbs
- ☐ Testimonials
- ☐ Interview Questions
- ☐ Q&A
- ☐ Contact Details

Links

- ☐ Website
- ☐ Book Page
- ☐ Book Buy Links (Amazon, B&N, etc.)
- ☐ Social Media Links
- ☐ Video Clips (speakers)
- ☐ Sound Clips (speakers)

THE NEXT STEP—BE MY GUEST

If you've arrived on this page after reading this entire book—thank you and congratulations. I can't wait to hear of your success stories as you implement the tools in this guide and take your book on its own audio tour.

Now, this is where the average writer stops. The average writer reads a book, gets inspired but ultimately takes no action.

Simply by making it to the end of this book tells me you're not average. You have a message to share with the world, and I'm passionate about helping you do that.

I hope you feel motivated to take action and get started transforming your book promotion into a completely fun audio tour that fuels your business and helps you get your message into the hands of the appropriate readers for your book.

As you now know, by implementing the Media Kit Checklist outlined in this book, you can be a much higher quality guest for your book's audio tour.

I'd love to hear from you.

As I said, there's truly nothing I enjoy more than working with writers and business owners whose passion runs so deep they literally wrote the book on the subject!

If that's you and you'd like to further explore how my team and I can help you implement Taking Your Book on an Audio Tour for yourself, then I invite you to take the next step and complete an Audio Tour survey.

This short survey will help me understand what you do, what your goals are and if an audio tour is right for you. It takes no more than 5 minutes to complete, and of course, I keep all of your information completely confidential. To get started, visit:

AuthorPodcasting.com/apply

Once your survey is submitted, I will be notified and will review it personally. If I think there's a good fit and we can genuinely help you, my team will reach out and schedule a call. This call is all about helping you decide if working together to create your own high-quality media kit and start you on an audio tour is a good fit for both of us. It would be an honor for me and my entire team to guide you and your book on this audio journey and to be one of the first podcasters on your tour. Unfortunately, we're not able to work with everyone, so this is not a sales call. It's more of a two-way interview to make sure we agree this is a good match.

Sound good?

Ok, it's time to close this book and take massive action on making it happen.

I look forward to hearing from you, and more importantly, working together to transform the way you are currently using your book to grow your readership.

To your continued success and to getting your book into the hands of your readers,

Janine Bolon

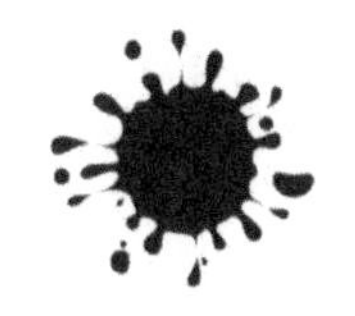

ABOUT JANINE BOLON

Janine Bolon is an unwilling author who started writing the books in 2005. She was told she wasn't a good writer throughout college and was stunned to discover that her students at University loved her writing style. Since that time of writing course books and programs for her mentally active classes, she has written nonfiction books in four different genres while establishing her own online University, four podcast programs, and continues to publish a book a year.

To learn more about Janine's many programs, visit her company's website at **The8Gates.com**.

PODCAST RESOURCES

Since my company, The8Gates, produces four podcast programs, I invite you to listen to them to see which one would be best for your book's promotion and your message.

The Writers Hour |
Creative Conversations

This podcast focuses on the process of writing books, how you managed to create a book despite your busy schedule and life responsibilities. This is a great show to mentor other writers with your specific style of writing as well as the systems you used to get the book completed with all the other demands your life has on your time. Visit **AuthorPodcasting.com.**

The Thriving Solopreneur Podcast

Do you wish to mentor fellow business professionals in their work? This is the show for you. Here is where we assist folks who are just starting their own business and need some guidance from folks who made the jump into self-employment with success. If you're a thriving solopreneur, please consider being our guest. Visit **JanineBolon.com.**

3 Minute Money Tip!

This mini-podcast gives our guests exactly three minutes to speak without interruption or questions to deliver a money tip that they think will be of service to our listeners. You don't need to be an expert at money, just something useful that helped you when you saw challenges in your cash flow. Visit **FinancialFirstResponse.com.**

The Practical Mystic Show

This is our longest running show (five years as of this printing). If you are an energy worker, light worker or have written about your experiences of near death, health transformation or insights beyond the veil, we'd love to have you as a guest. Visit **ThePracticalMystics.com.**

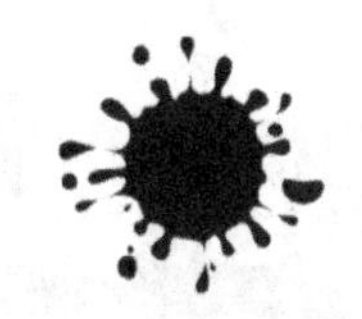

CONNECT WITH ME

Tell me about the book you're writing and where you are in your journey of being an author. I'm an excellent listener and would relish the opportunity to hear how you are doing. Be sure to connect with me on LinkedIn:

LinkedIn.com/in/janinebolon

READER BONUS

Your investment in this book entitles you to a very special gift that is the foundation of Author Podcasting™

It is a seven-part recording of an exclusive training, “Building Your Media Kit,” where attendees invested $197 to participate, and you can have it as my gift to you!

The training goes into greater detail on how to make your media kit in Google documents with over-the-shoulder tutorials and explains the importance of having active links and hashtags for your business and social media marketing.

DOWNLOAD TODAY!

AuthorPodcasting.com/readerbonus